Stop and Run

A play

Diana Raffle

Samuel French — London
www.samuelfrench-london.co.uk

STOP AND RUN

First performed at Langley Village Hall, Langley, near Maidstone, Kent, on 11th July 2009, with the following cast:

Eileen Dodds	Sheila Veitch
Tracy Dodds	Jan Hooper
Jackie Prentiss	Nic Grin
Kevin Prentiss	Scott Raffle
Raymond White	Joe Bailey

COPYRIGHT INFORMATION
(See also page ii)

CHARACTERS

Eileen Dodds, late 60s
Tracy Dodds, Eileen's daughter, 40s
Jackie Prentiss, Eileen's daughter, 40s or 50s
Kevin Prentiss, Jackie's husband, 40s or 50s
Raymond White, Eileen's new partner, late 60s

SYNOPSIS OF SCENES

The action of the play takes place in Tracy's living-room

Time — the present

Other plays by Diana Raffle
published by Samuel French Ltd

Blue Suede Blues
Camp Confidence

STOP AND RUN

Tracy's living-room. Daytime

A telephone rings and rings. Eventually, Tracy stumbles on with two full Co-op shopping bags. She drops one and oranges fall out. She picks up the phone

Tracy Hello? Hello? (*She puts the phone down*) Bloody hell.

She starts to pick up the oranges and the phone rings again. She picks up the receiver

(*Into the phone; shouting*) Hello? … Who? … What flowers? … I haven't ordered any flowers. … They're for what? … The wedding? What wedding?

The doorbell rings

Look, I think that there must be some mistake. I got married ten years ago and I ain't planning to do it again, thanks. … Yes, that's my number. … Well, you must have written it down wrong or something. … How the hell should I know?

The doorbells rings again

Anyway, I've got to go. Someone's at the door and my navels just rolled under the settee. … Yeah, fine, if I hear anything about a wedding I'll let you know. (*She hangs up the phone*) Probably thought twice about it.

She picks up an orange and exits to the door

Tracy enters with Jackie, who wears a miniskirt and is heavily made up, though she is in her forties or fifties

Jackie About bloody time. I've been freezing my bum off in that hallway of yours. You ought to provide something for your visitors.

Tracy pulls off a pair of trousers from her airer and tosses them to Jackie

Tracy There, that should cover your frostbite.

Jackie Trousers? You must be joking. Kevin likes me to wear clothes that show off my assets.

Tracy Nobody wants their assets frozen though, do they?

Jackie You're just jealous 'cause you got Nan's veins.

Tracy As far as I am aware, Nan took her veins with her.

Jackie Oh, you know what I mean. Nan's varicose veins.

Tracy I bloody didn't.

Jackie Oh, yes, you did. Your legs look like Mr Universe's biceps on a hot day.

Tracy What do you want?

Jackie Oh, that's nice, isn't it? I've hardly seen you for weeks and all you can say is "what do you want?"

Tracy Well? I am busy, you know. I do have a life.

Jackie Oh, yeah, I can see that. (*Noticing the oranges*) What have you been doing? Practising your juggling?

Tracy The phone was ringing as I walked in the door and I dropped them. Actually, I shouldn't have bothered picking it up. It was only some snotty cow from the florists.

Jackie So you know?

Tracy Know what?

Jackie About the wedding.

Tracy What wedding?

Jackie I thought you said that the florist's rang you this morning.

Tracy Yeah, they did, but I told them that they must have the wrong number.

Jackie Mum hasn't told you, has she?

Tracy Told me what? What the hell is going on?

Jackie It's Mum. She's met some bloke on holiday and she's getting married.

Tracy What?

Jackie I thought that would make you stand up.

Tracy I *was* bleeding standing up. But now I want to sit down. You'd better tell me what's going on.

Jackie I just did. Mum went on holiday and met a bloke.

Tracy A bloke?

Jackie Raymond.

Tracy Raymond.

Jackie Yes, Raymond. He's a bingo caller.

Tracy I might have guessed.

Jackie Anyway, when she came back Kevin picked her up from the coach station and she tells him that she and Raymond are going to get married.

Tracy When?

Jackie Next week.

Tracy Next week?

Jackie What's wrong with you today? I feel like I'm shouting down a well.

Tracy Does anyone know this Raymond?

Jackie Only Mum.

Tracy So you haven't met him then?

Jackie No. I s'pose he's still in Scarborough calling the bingo.

Tracy Does Dad know?

Jackie Not yet. Kevin says we ought to tell him soon though.

Tracy Well, I'm not bloody telling him.

Jackie You are his favourite.

Tracy So was Mum until he ran off with Ivy from the chippy.

Jackie That was just a fling.

Tracy Mum didn't see it that way. She only sent him off for a portion of chips and two pickled eggs. She didn't see him again for five years.

Jackie Nan always said Ivy took the takeaway sign too literally.

Tracy Mum's never been the same since.

Jackie All I remember was waiting for a chip butty and ending up with a marge sandwich.

Tracy Yeah, well, we went without a lot of stuff after he left.

Jackie I know, but that was years ago and he's been doing his best to get back with her, you know he has. He was the one that gave her the money for this holiday so as she could think about them.

Tracy It doesn't look like she's given "them" much thought, does it?

Jackie Dad's going to go mad.

Tracy So why should I tell him? Why can't Mum tell him? She's the one who's getting married.

Jackie She's frightened that he'll get violent.

Tracy All the more reason for me not to stick my nose in.

Jackie You're just being bitter.

Tracy Bitter? How do you work that one out?

Jackie Because you've got this thing about getting married.

Tracy That's rubbish.

Jackie No, it's not. Ever since you and Sean split up, you've been funny.

Tracy Broke, depressed, lonely and bitter, yes — funny, no.

Jackie That's what I meant. You don't like weddings anymore, do you?

Tracy No, I don't, but that doesn't mean to say that I am bothered if anyone else wants to try one.

Jackie Good. So you can tell Dad.

Tracy I didn't say that, did I? God, Jackie, why should I do all the dirty work? If Mum's getting married she should tell Dad, not us. She's over sixty, she can do what the hell she wants, can't she?

Jackie Maybe she's going funny in the head.

Tracy Or perhaps she thinks she's in love.

Jackie My Kevin thinks this Raymond might be after Mum's money.

Tracy She's hardly Ivana Trump.

Jackie Nan left her a bit though, didn't she?

Tracy A bit of what? Certainly not a bloody sense of humour.

Jackie You know what I mean. She left a few bits.

Tracy You were at that solicitors, Jack. All Nan left was a battered old vanity case and her teeth.

Jackie Which she gave to you.

Tracy Oh, for God's sake Jackie, I said you could have them. I didn't want them. They're hardly likely to fit me in thirty years' time, are they?

Jackie Nan didn't like to see nothing go to waste.

Tracy There are limits. Besides, I haven't got them anymore.

Jackie What did you do with them?

Tracy I gave them to the funeral directors, so Nan could enter the next life without spitting over Saint Peter.

Jackie That's nice, you could have told me. I would have liked to have had them. Just for sentimental reasons.

Tracy How can you be sentimental about a pair of teeth?

Jackie Yeah, well, that's easy for you to say when you've been left them. I didn't get anything.

Tracy And I'm telling you that there wasn't anything worth having.

Jackie Mum said that Nan always put her savings under the bed and not in the bank 'cause she didn't trust them, and that old vanity case was under her bed.

Tracy Knowing Nan, all that's in that case will be her truss and the necklace Granddad made for her out of his gallstones.

Jackie If that's all that was in it then why is she so careful to carry it around with her all the time? Kevin reckons if it is full of Nan's savings that's what this Raymond bloke is after.

Tracy And I'm supposed to be the cynic?

Jackie She even took it to Scarborough with her an' all. My Kevin said she had it when she got on the coach, and unless she was planning on dressing up in Nan's truss and flinging the gallstones round her neck on party night, I reckon she's got something else in there.

Tracy Well, even in the completely unlikely event of Nan leaving Mum a few quid in the vanity case, Mum isn't stupid enough to tell this bloke about it, is she?

Jackie How do you know? This Raymond could have seen her coming and now he thinks he's on to a good thing.

Tracy Or maybe he just likes her.

Jackie You are kidding me. The last time I saw her smile was when next door's cat died.

Tracy It was only a suggestion.

Jackie Kevin says she must be on the rebound.

Tracy Blimey, that's some delayed reaction. Dad left her thirty years ago.

Jackie She's so lonely, I don't know what she's capable of, really. I think that was why she started looking at Kenny.

Tracy Who the hell's Kenny?

Jackie The short, hairy bloke that fixed her boiler.

Tracy Mum never told me.

Jackie I'm not saying anything happened like, but I always noticed things were a bit warmer in her flat after she'd met him.

Tracy That's probably because he'd fixed her boiler.

Jackie She never admitted anything, but after she found out he was married to that tart in the tanning shop she went and switched to Seeboard.

Tracy Well, she was better off without him then, wasn't she?

Jackie You're as bad as her.

Tracy Where's Mum now?

Jackie Kevin's gone to pick her up. He said he was going to do a bit of digging on the way back.

Tracy Oh, great, Inspector bleeding Frost is on the case, eh?

Jackie So, what do you think? Kevin reckons that if he's not after Mum's money then maybe he's looking for somewhere to doss.

Tracy But I thought this Raymond has got a job. You said that he was a bingo caller.

Jackie Yes, but his work's seasonal, isn't it? Like those blokes who dress up as Santa. He only works in the holiday season. Kevin says that he won't earn much and he probably lives in one of those *chalets*. He might not have anywhere else to go in the winter.

Tracy Kevin seems to know a lot about it.

Jackie Yeah, well, I bought him the entire series of *Hi De Hi* on DVD for his last birthday, so he knows about them holiday camps.

Tracy Why didn't I think of that?

Jackie He's very observant, my Kevin, you know. He reckons this Raymond might only be looking for somebody to keep him warm through the winter.

Tracy Can't you give him Kenny's number?

Jackie Tracy, you're not taking this seriously. What are we going to do?

Tracy What are you asking me for? Hasn't Kevin got a plan?

Jackie He told me to ask you. So?

Tracy Talk to her, I s'pose.

The doorbell rings

Jackie Great, well here's your chance.

Tracy What are you on about? Is that Mum at the door?

Jackie Kevin said he might drop her off here for a bit.

Tracy A bit of what?

Jackie A bit of a chat.

Tracy You mean you knew that he was bringing her round here and you didn't tell me?

Jackie What does it matter? You said you were gonna speak to her anyway.

Tracy I meant we were gonna speak to her.

Jackie Well I can't, Kevin says that I've ——

Tracy I don't give a monkey's about what Kevin says, Jack. Stuff him, for once in your life. You're the ones getting your knickers in a twist about Mum, so you can stop here until we've sorted things out.

Jackie But Kevin says I've got to leave it up to you.

Tracy Well, Tracy says shut up and sit down.

Jackie looks unnerved and sits down

Tracy storms off to open the door

A few seconds later Tracy enters, followed by Eileen. She is dressed in a long, drab coat. Her hair is shoved under a headscarf and she is carrying a bag and clutching a vanity case. She looks permanently miserable, curls her lip and sniffs a lot

Jackie Oh, hello Mum. You're looking well.

Tracy I can only see her eyes.

Jackie Yes, well, they look … brighter. That holiday must have done you some good.

Eileen It did.

Jackie You sound different too. Have you done something to your teeth?

Tracy Why don't you sit down, Mum, so we can have a chat?

Eileen I'm not sitting down until you let Raymond in.

Jackie You mean he's here?

Tracy You didn't say anything. I didn't know he was outside.

Eileen He's not, he's in the car with Jackie's Kevin. I just wanted to make sure that he was going to be welcome if I asked him in.

Tracy Well, of course he would be welcome. What do you take us for, Mum?

Eileen I know you well enough and I know that you'll have been discussing my wedding.

Jackie As if, eh Tracy?

Eileen You mean you haven't been talking about it then?

Jackie Maybe. Tracy might have mentioned it.

Eileen Only this is the first time I've been happy since I met your father and I don't want nothing to interfere with this, all right? Do I make myself clear?

Tracy As a bell, Mum.

Eileen Right then, I'll give him the gesture.

Tracy Eh?

Eileen I said to him to wait until I had given him the gesture to come in.

Tracy I'd better open the door then.

Tracy exits

Jackie This is all a bit sudden, isn't it, Mum?

Eileen Not for me.

Jackie Yeah, but you hardly know him.

Eileen At my age, how long do you think I should spend getting to know him?

Jackie Is he nice looking? I mean, is that what you see in him?

Eileen Nope.

Jackie Well, what do you think he sees in you then?

Eileen He don't see anything. He's blind.

Jackie Blind? Then how's he going to see your gesture?

Eileen I told your Kevin to give him a thump when I waved. That should do it.

Jackie I can't believe all this.

Eileen He may be blind, but you should hear him call the bingo. I've never seen anyone say them words like he does.

Jackie Pardon me for stating the obvious Mum, but how does he read the numbers?

Eileen He's got special balls. They've got little bumps on instead of the numbers. He sort of runs his fingers over them and reads them like that.

Jackie That's amazing.

Eileen He says "brighton line" like no one I've ever heard and when he called out "sweet sixteen" I nearly forgot to mark it off. He's got a voice like velvet on that microphone.

Jackie Kevin says he probably won't be working during the winter.

Eileen Why, he hasn't done his back in again, has he?

Jackie No, not Kevin, I meant Raymond. Perhaps he won't be working because the holiday camp shuts.

Eileen Well, for once your Kevin's right. That's why Raymond's going for an interview next week, at the Palace.

Tracy enters with Raymond. He is dressed in a suit and a colourful bow tie, and is wearing dark glasses

Raymond, come and sit over here, love.

Raymond No problem, my little dove. Let me get comfy, then you can introduce me to your beautiful daughters.

Jackie (*loudly*) Hello Raymond, my name is Jackie.

Eileen There's no need to talk like that. Raymond's blind, not deaf.

Raymond Now, now, sweetheart, Jackie's only being thoughtful. Where's your hand, so I can give you a kiss? (*He takes Jackie's hand and gives it a kiss*) Oh, you smell gorgeous. If I were twenty years younger …

Eileen You'd still be too old. You met Tracy at the door, didn't you?

Raymond The fair Tracy, that's right. Although she didn't let me take any liberties on the mat. Not much of a "naughty forty" are you, eh girl!

Tracy Eh?

Eileen It's a bingo call. He's only joking with you. He jokes with everyone, don't you, Raymond?

Raymond The world needs to smile a bit more, that's what I say.

Jackie My Kevin says —

Tracy So, when did you decide to get married, then?

Raymond Snakes alive, you're not backward in coming forward, are you, Tracy?

Eileen Tracy doesn't mean anything by it, do you, Tracy?

Raymond Don't worry. I don't take offence that easily, you know, and I realize your Tracy is just looking out for her mum. Isn't that right?

Tracy I'm sorry. I didn't mean to sound rude. It's just all so sudden.

Eileen Not as sudden as your dad's departure.

Jackie I'm sure Raymond doesn't want to hear about Dad, Mum.

Raymond Now, don't you worry, your mum's told me everything. In bingo terms we would have said he went "straight on through".

Eileen More like he got distracted by two fat ladies. One of them caught him good and proper.

Raymond Well, he was a fool, wasn't he?

Tracy Would you like a cup of tea, Raymond?

Raymond A number three? That would be lovely, Tracy.

Tracy Do you take sugar?

Raymond "One little duck", please Tracy.

Eileen That means two.

Jackie I thought he said one.

Eileen It's a bingo call.

Raymond "Two little ducks" is twenty-two, see, so one is two.

Jackie Right.

Eileen You'll get the hang of it.

Tracy I wouldn't bank on it. Mum? Cup of tea?

Eileen Yeah, that'd be nice. Then we can sit down and talk about what you're going to wear to our wedding next week.

Jackie Let me put the kettle on, eh. I'll let you know when it's boiling, Trace.

Jackie exits to the kitchen

The doorbell rings

Tracy Who's that now?
Raymond Sounds like a "knock at the door".
Eileen That's number four.
Tracy I'd better get it.
Eileen I expect it's Jackie's Kevin. He won't want to be left sitting in his car.
Raymond Keen to know what's going on, is he?
Eileen No, his heater's broken.

Tracy exits

Raymond So, how am I doing? Do you reckon they're softening or are they going to eat this "man alive"?
Eileen It doesn't matter what they think. I'm happy. That's all. They'll have to live with it. Are you all right?
Raymond I wouldn't mind going to the lav.
Eileen Oh, right, well I'll show you where it is.

Raymond and Eileen get up and she begins to lead him off

Tracy enters with Kevin. He is dressed in a shell suit with trainers, is unshaven, and his hair looks scruffy, as though he's just woken up

Tracy It was Kevin.
Kevin (*nodding towards them*) Eileen. Raymond.
Eileen Raymond needs the lav.
Tracy Oh, fine. Does he need any help?
Raymond Don't you worry girl, these might be new surroundings but some things can always be found in the same place. Know what I mean?

Eileen I'll show him where you keep the soap.
Tracy Right.

Raymond and Eileen exit to the bathroom

Kevin sits down

I was just about to make a pot of tea, Kevin. You want one?
Kevin Yeah, thanks. Two sugars please.
Tracy "One little duck" it is.
Kevin Eh?

Tracy exits

Kevin looks at the vanity case and picks it up

Jackie walks back in and Kevin drops the case

Jackie What are you doing, Kevin?
Kevin I was trying to take a look at that bloody case, only you came in on me.
Jackie Well don't blame me, I didn't know that you were snooping.
Kevin I wasn't snooping.
Jackie What would you call it, then?
Kevin Look, that flipping bag has not left your mum's side since your nan died last year. She takes it everywhere with her.
Jackie She hasn't taken it to the loo.
Kevin That's 'cause this bloke has got her head all mixed up. She never would have let this case out of her sight before he came on the scene.
Jackie Tracy thinks there's nothing in it.
Kevin Yeah, well she didn't see what I saw, did she?
Jackie What did you see, then?

Eileen walks back in and goes to the case

Eileen I'd better stay outside the door with him, he won't know his way back to the lounge.

Eileen picks up the case and exits to the bathroom

Tracy enters with a tray of tea

Tracy What's going on?

Kevin You see, she won't go anywhere without that case.

Jackie Kevin saw something, didn't you, Kevin?

Tracy Like what?

Kevin It was when your mum got on the coach to go to Scarborough. She hadn't bought her ticket at the desk because of the queue, and her leg was giving her gip, so she says she's going to get her ticket from the driver.

Tracy So what?

Kevin Well, she puts down her bag and opens up that vanity case, just a bit, so the driver couldn't see, but I was standing behind her waiting to wave her off and I caught sight of a bundle of notes.

Jackie Letters?

Kevin No, banknotes.

Tracy Maybe it's Mum's savings.

Jackie Mum hasn't got any savings. That's why Dad had to pay for this holiday.

Tracy Perhaps that's just what she told him.

Kevin I'm telling you, that case is full of money.

Jackie But what if this Raymond knows that?

Kevin Well, it's obvious, isn't it? That's what he's after.

Tracy I hate to burst your little bubble Kevin, but if the bloke's blind, how is he supposed to have seen any money?

Kevin She must have told him about it.

Jackie Why?

Kevin So he'd marry her.

Jackie Mum wouldn't do that.

Kevin Why not, she's lonely as hell, and she'd do anything to get back at your dad.

Tracy But what sort of bloke would get married for a few pounds?

Kevin It wasn't just a few quid in that case, Tracy.

Jackie And we don't know what sort of bloke this Mr Clickety-Clack is, do we?

Tracy Click. It's Clickety-Click.

Jackie Who cares? What I want to know is if he's trying to make off with our inheritance.

Kevin She should have told you about it.

Tracy I can't believe she didn't.

Jackie She always was tight.

Eileen enters

Eileen What's wrong with you lot? You look like you've seen a ghost.

Tracy Er … here's your tea.

Eileen Ta.

Jackie Where's Raymond?

Eileen In the lav. He reckons his tummy's a bit upset from the journey.

Kevin So, have you told your husband then, Eileen?

Eileen Ex-husband, and it's no business of yours.

Jackie Mum! Kevin was only asking.

Eileen I know what Kevin was doing. You all want me to tell your dad so he can muscle his way in and ruin it, don't you?

Tracy Mum, no one wants to spoil anything.

Eileen Oh, yes, you do. Of course you do. You'd rather find out I was going do-lally than think that I was getting married to some bloke from the holiday camp.

Kevin It's all a bit sudden, I s'pose.

Eileen Sudden? Sending my husband out for some pickled eggs and never seeing him again was sudden. Finding out he's spent all our savings was sudden. Getting evicted with two kids was sudden.

Tracy We know it wasn't easy, Mum.

Eileen You don't know anything. I wasn't always like this, you know. I had my looks and a decent figure. When Vinnie came along I thought it was all going to be OK, he'd look after me, and so I looked after him. I washed, cooked, cleaned — nearly died giving him two kids. You name it, I did it, whenever or whatever he wanted, and look where it got me, eh?

Jackie Dad knows he didn't treat you very well.

Eileen He was a bastard to me and you. He never paid a bleeding penny in maintenance. Who do you think paid for your winter coats or the shoes on your feet, eh?

Tracy Look, Mum, we're not trying to upset you.

Eileen But you are, you are upsetting me. Look at me. Don't you realize that I have been unhappy that long I can't even remember what it's like to wake up and not feel like topping myself? I don't care what I wear, or what my hair's like. I don't even bother cooking much for myself anymore. If it comes in a tin, I eat it. I sit for hours watching folks arguing on the tele and then when they're all finished I sit and stare into space.

Jackie But you wanted to go on holiday.

Eileen The only reason I went on that bloody trip was 'cause I couldn't stand another birthday here. Folks I never see any other day popping in with cards and a new scarf 'cause no one knew what to buy such a miserable old cow anymore. I didn't want to be me this year, I didn't want to be here.

Tracy Are you saying that you care now?

Jackie Do you love him then, Mum?

Eileen Love? No, I don't love him, he just makes me smile, and when he's about I don't feel quite so tired. Love is something I've done without for years but company is what I want more than anything. Loneliness is what's killing me.

Jackie Well, how about we came round more often?

Eileen A couple of visits isn't the same. I want a man's company, someone to make a cup of tea for and iron a few shirts for. I want to be needed again, be useful, have a bit of purpose to my days and then when we sit down in the evening, I've got company, someone to watch the tele with or do one of them big jigsaws. Look, I even had my hair done. (*She takes off her headscarf*)

Jackie Blimey, Mum. He has cheered you up.

Tracy But why marry him, Mum? Couldn't you just live together?

Eileen I want to get wed. He promised me that if I give him the money then he'll marry me. That'll shut Vinnie and his family up.

Tracy What money?

Eileen Your nan left it to me, after she died.

Jackie What did I tell you?

Tracy Are you telling me that you are paying Raymond to marry you?

Kevin You can't do that.

Eileen Why can't I? My mother left it to me, so I can do whatever I like with it.

Jackie Isn't it illegal or something? To pay for a bloke, I mean.

Eileen People pay for them designer babies, don't they?

Jackie Yeah, but you're hardly designer.

Tracy Mum, you need that money.

Eileen I need Raymond more.

Jackie How much have you got?

Eileen That don't matter.

Jackie Yes it does. I want to know how much you are giving this bloke.

Eileen All right then, I'll tell you, although I can't see it making you any happier. I'm giving him five thousand.

Tracy Five thousand pounds? Mum you can't do that. It was Nan's and she wouldn't have wanted you to give it away to a stranger.

Eileen But he won't be a stranger, will he, because he'll be my husband.

Kevin By the time the ink's dry on the certificate, I'd put money on him being a bloody stranger. (*He wanders across to the other side of the room*)

Eileen He won't be running anywhere. He promised me. Raymond's not like your father, he's different. He thinks about things, about things that make me happy. Look what he bought me the day after we met. It's them Seekers that I used to like. No one's bought me any music in years. Only I don't have one of them players.

Eileen gets a CD out of her bag and passes it to Tracy. It's "A World of Our Own" by The Seekers

Tracy If you kept that money you could buy yourself one.

Eileen It was all the thing when you were born. It takes me right back. Why don't you put it on for me? I want to hear it.

Kevin It's hardly the time to go reminiscing.
Eileen It's just the time. Put it on, Tracy, I want to hear it.

Tracy puts on the CD

Kevin This is bloody ridiculous. You can't be serious, Eileen.
Eileen It isn't actually any of your business what I do. All I know is
that Nan wanted me to be happy and this is going to make me happy.
Don't you want me to be happy, is that it?
Jackie Not if it's costing five grand to do it.
Eileen Well, you'll just have to get used to it, won't you, because I'm
marrying Raymond and nothing you or anyone else can say is going
to change that.
Kevin I wouldn't be too sure about that.
Eileen What do you mean?
Kevin Your Raymond has just gone out the front door.
Eileen He's what! Raymond?

Eileen runs out

(*Off*) Raymond.

The music gets louder

Kevin I'll go after her.

Kevin runs off

Jackie Oh, my God.
Tracy Mum? Mum?

Tracy exits

Jackie He's probably just gone through the wrong door. Mum?
Mum!

Jackie exits

Eventually Eileen enters and sits down. A few moments later Jackie enters and turns off the music

Jackie He's gone.

Kevin enters

Kevin I thought you said he was blind.
Eileen He was.
Kevin Well, he must have had a miraculous recovery in the bog, because he's just driven off in my car.
Jackie Oh my God.

Tracy enters

Tracy I couldn't stop him.
Jackie He's only gone and taken our car.
Tracy I know.
Kevin (*to Eileen*) This is all your fault, you stupid old bag. What the hell were you thinking of, bringing him home with you?
Tracy Kevin, shut up. Can't you see Mum's in a state?
Kevin It's all right for her, she hasn't just had her car nicked, has she?
Jackie Where's the vanity case?
Tracy Mum had it.
Kevin She took it out with her when she was helping bloody Raymond.
Jackie Mum? Did you leave the case outside?

Eileen sits impassively

Kevin Give me the phone, Jack. I'm going to call the police and then you can call the doctor and get her put away.
Tracy Don't you dare speak to my mum like that, you prat. (*She grabs the phone*)
Jackie Tracy, my Kevin is not a prat.
Eileen He took it.

Tracy What?

Eileen The miserable bastard took my case. I left it in the hallway, and he took it.

Tracy Oh, God, Mum. I could have paid for my college place. I've been having to scrimp and save just to pay the fees and all the time you were sitting on a fortune. What were you thinking?

Jackie All that money. We could have had a new washing machine, ours only spins when it feels like it nowadays.

Eileen I didn't think.

Kevin You stupid, stupid woman. Give me the bloody phone.

Jackie Kevin!

Kevin What? What do you expect me to say? The woman's lost the plot.

Tracy What's the point? You might as well leave her alone.

Kevin Leave her alone? I can't wait to leave her alone, only if you hadn't noticed I can't go anywhere until someone brings back my bloody car.

Jackie Oh God, I'd forgotten about the car.

Eileen I trusted him.

Tracy Why? You haven't trusted anyone in your life before.

Jackie Not to mention the fact that our kids haven't had a decent holiday in years.

Eileen It's not my fault.

Kevin Of course it's your bloody fault. If you hadn't brought him home none of this would have happened. Anybody else goes away to a holiday camp, they bring home a stick of rock or the runs, but not you, no, you had to go and bring the bloody bingo caller with you. He must have seen you coming. God, I can even sympathize with Vinnie now.

Jackie Dad always said you were soft in the head.

Eileen How dare you! All I did was trust someone, and look where it's got me. You don't care about me, you don't care how I feel. I've only ever trusted two men in my life and they've both crapped on me, and all you care about is yourselves, your car, and the kids. Whose fault is it that those kids haven't had a proper holiday, eh?

Jackie Don't you bring that up again.

Eileen What, the fact that your precious bloody Kevin has spent every
  penny that he's ever earned in the pub.

Jackie That's not true.

Kevin You better watch your tongue.

Tracy Mum, please.

Eileen What? Pretend it's not true, shall we? Pretend that your
  husband didn't find you in bed with your college friend? Oh, yes, I
  knew all about it. Your Sean made sure I did. You sit there and make
  us all think that you've been treated badly when it was you doing the
  dirty all along and as for you, Jackie, well you married a drunk and
  we all know it. So don't you dare look at me and accuse me of not
  giving you money for stuff, that money was mine. The first time I'd
  ever been given any money in my life and it was for me, not you,
  or your kids or for you to go and sleep with another professor. Me.
  None of you care if I'm dead or alive. All you ever think about is
  yourselves, so if it's gone then I'm glad, because at least none of you
  got your grabbing, selfish hands on it.

Kevin I'm gonna kill her.

*Kevin steps up to Eileen, who starts to scream. Jackie and Tracy scream
and try to hold him back. Eileen tries to escape but Kevin has her by
the throat. Jackie hits him on the head with a magazine and he staggers
back, then Tracy accidentally hits Jackie. Kevin starts to throttle Tracy.
Jackie jumps on his back and he spins around*

*The telephone rings and they all stop and look at the phone. Tracy
goes over to it*

Tracy (*into the phone*) Hello? … Oh, hello, Dad. (*She turns and makes
  a worried face*)

Eileen and Jackie sit down. Kevin smoothes down his hair

  Yes, Mum's home. Did you want to speak to her? … Oh, OK,
  that sounds nice. … What? You've just passed Kevin's car at the
  station? … Oh, right, yeah, he lent it to a friend. He's just off to pick
  it up now.

Jackie At least we've not lost the car.

Tracy Oh, right, OK. I'll tell her. … Bye, Dad. Bye.

Kevin Well, what did he say?

Tracy He's coming to pick Mum up. He wants to take her out to the pub.

Jackie I hope he's paying.

Kevin I'd better go and check out the car.

Eileen I'd better get my coat done up.

Tracy So that's it? You're just going to go out with Dad now?

Eileen That's it.

Jackie So nothing's changed, after all.

Eileen I suppose it hasn't. (*She puts her headscarf back on*)

Tracy And everything Nan left you has gone.

Eileen Not everything. (*She bares her teeth*)

Jackie I don't believe it. You're wearing Nan's teeth.

Eileen I wasn't going to let them go. Nan would have wanted me to have passed them on.

Kevin Oh, well that's a bloody comfort.

Eileen I'll wait at the door for your dad. He likes to get away sharp, especially if he's going to the pub.

Tracy Fine, you go. I'll just sit here and pretend that nothing's happened.

Eileen What do you want me to do?

Tracy I don't know. Cry, maybe get a bit upset. The bloke you thought was going to marry you next week has just scampered with your bloody inheritance.

Jackie Our inheritance, more like.

Eileen Well, there ain't much I can do about that now, is there? The wedding's off, and I'll thank you all to keep your mouths shut about this around your father.

Jackie So, what are we going to do if the florist calls back?

Eileen Tell them to send the flowers. Your dad'll pay.

Jackie You mean you're going to marry Dad now?

Eileen If he asks me.

Kevin I don't believe this. Have you got anyone else up your sleeve if he doesn't pop the question?

Jackie Oh, shut up, Kev.

Tracy But you don't love him, Mum.

Eileen Don't suppose he loves me either, but we're both too old to go looking elsewhere now. My last chance just walked off with all my worldly goods. So now's not the time to be choosy. Besides, your nan used to say, life was all about taking your chance when it showed itself. Raymond took his and now I'm taking mine. He never got my name right anyway.

Kevin He got five grand though, didn't he? He must be laughing.

Eileen Oh, I doubt it. It was all them old notes, see. Nan had been saving them for years. I didn't realize they weren't worth anything until I tried to buy a sandwich in the camp cafe.

Jackie You mean he can't spend it?

Eileen Oh, there was a few of the new notes, but I paid for the coach with two of them, the rest is nothing more than old paper.

Jackie So you never really had five grand at all?

Eileen Oh, yes, I did. Just not the sort of five grand that you could spend. It's funny what money does to folks, isn't it? Whilst I had that case, you all wanted me, as soon as it's gone, only your dad wants me. So, I'll take my chances. Just like Raymond took his.

Tracy At least you got a CD out of him.

Eileen I reckon he thought that it was a good investment. At least I can still play it even if he can't spend his cash. Well, see you next week then, Trace.

Tracy Yeah. See you next week, Mum. Oh, hang on, I forgot to give you this. It's for your birthday.

Tracy hands Eileen a present. Eileen unwraps it and holds up her new headscarf

Eileen A scarf. Ta, it's very nice, love.

Tracy Back to normal, eh?

Eileen Probably best.

Tracy Maybe next year we'll get you one of those CD players, eh?

Jackie We'll chip in.

Eileen I'll hold you to that.

Tracy And if you get lonely, you can call me.

Jackie And me. We didn't know.

Eileen I know that. Trouble is, loneliness don't give you a rash so's people can see it. It's like a silent killer.

Tracy But you and Dad …

Eileen It's something. It's something different, something I haven't got at the moment and that's a lot better than nothing.

Jackie I think I hear Dad's car.

Kevin Speaking of which, we'd better go down and get our car back.

Jackie Right, see you then.

Tracy Yeah, see you.

Jackie Remember what I said Mum, about calling.

Eileen I will, Jackie. I will.

Kevin and Jackie exit

Eileen (*changing her headscarf*) There, what do you think?

Tracy It don't look that much different to the last one.

Eileen Then it's fine. Sometimes change ain't always for the best.

Tracy Why don't we go for a night out some time? I'd take you.

Eileen Yeah, why not? That'd be nice. Perhaps we could take Jackie an' all. I didn't mean to be so hard on her.

Tracy I know. So, where shall we go?

Eileen Do you know what, I don't really mind as long as it ain't the bleeding bingo. Ta-da, love.

Tracy Yeah, ta-da, Mum. Ta-da.

The Lights fade to Black-out

FURNITURE AND PROPERTY LIST

On stage: Telephone
Airer. *On it*: trousers
CD player
Gift-wrapped headscarf
Magazine

Off stage: Co-op shopping bags containing oranges (**Tracy**)
Tray of tea (**Tracy**)
Vanity case, bag containing CD (**Eileen**)

LIGHTING PLOT

Scene 1

To open: General interior lighting

| *Cue* 1 | **Tracy**: "Yeah, ta-da, Mum. Ta-da." | (Page 23) |
| | *Fade to Black-out* | |

EFFECTS PLOT

Printed by The Kingfisher Press, London NW10 7AS